return to ease

gently reconnect with your body's natural mobility and joy

Carolyn S. Barnes, LMT

Creative Development Editor:
Heather Doyle Fraser
www.beyondchangecoach.com

Copy Editor:
Martha Somes

Designer:
Barb Swartz
www.barbswartz.com

ISBN 978-0-9962583-0-2
Library of Congress Control Number: 2015915286

First Edition

Dublin, OH
www.return2ease.com

This book is dedicated to Kevin,
my beloved husband and partner in life,
who continues to believe in me
even when I doubt myself.
Every day I learn from your grace,
your kindness, your playful humor,
and your immense capacity
to act with love and integrity.
I love our life together.

Our deepest fear is not
that we are inadequate.

Our deepest fear is that
we are powerful beyond measure.
It is our light, not our darkness,
that most frightens us.

We ask ourselves, "Who am I to be
brilliant, gorgeous, talented, fabulous?"

Actually, who are you not to be?
And as we let our own light shine,
we unconsciously give other people
permission to do the same.

As we are liberated from our own fear,
our presence automatically
liberates others..

A Return to Love

table of contents

foreword 10

let's get prepared 15

let's get started 21

let's get centered 39

- grounding 44
- body scan 52
  - *body scan meditation* 55
- diaphragmatic breathing 60
- gratitude 66

let's get moving 75

- the foam roller 84
  - *shins release* 87
  - *hip flexor release* 88
  - *outside thigh release* 89
  - *low back release* 90
  - *front thigh release* 91
  - *neck release* 92
  - *shoulder blade release* 93
  - *chest opener with spinal release* 94
  - *buttock release* 95

the super pinky ball 98

foot roll 101

shoulder blade release 102

front shoulder opener 104

buttock release 105

movements and stretches 110

windmills 113

cat and cow poses 114

child's pose 115

alphabet balance 116

hanging low back release 117

figure 8 hip opener 118

swinging hip opener 119

spinal twist 120

let's expand your skills 125

acknowledgements 132

index of photographs 133

We delight in the beauty

of the butterfly,

but rarely admit

the changes

it has gone through

to achieve that beauty.

foreword

This book began healing long before it was published. In this way, it could be considered magical. After spending just a few minutes with it, you may come to agree.

Many things make this book magical.

Its author is a healer of shamanic caliber, with a deep love of nature, beauty, and unity. The combination produces powerful facilitation of happiness.

MAGIC.

Its title is also a mantra that immediately transforms one's mind-set and body-state. Thinking it, or stating it out loud, instantly realigns us with our calm center—the place of true power.

MAGIC.

Its wisdom quickly becomes evident because it creates a strong desire to come back. Our bodies begin to crave the practice.

MAGIC.

Its mission gives us what we need in order to do what we need to do. A rare path to self-empowerment opens equally to all. Everyone at every level benefits.

MAGIC.

Its spirit comes from many working in concert. Something inside everyone who was involved in the project was inspired. A harmony of individual thoughts, ideas, and visions coalesced around the recognition of something special.

MAGIC.

What you have in your hands holds its own type of magic for you, but the effects it will have on your life are very real.

PREPARE TO BE ENCHANTED.

Laura Walker

OracleReport.com, January 14, 2015, Washington, DC

A sacred choice is one that

does not seek to compensate for a wound,

but to heal it.

— Richard Vassallo

let's get prepared

Before you jump into the techniques, here are a few guidelines to keep you safe:

- Some of the techniques are more active than others and not necessarily suitable for everyone. Please use common sense and consult with your doctor before attempting any change in physical activity, especially if you suffer from high blood pressure, heart disease or any other disease or condition.

- If you feel dizzy, lightheaded, nauseous or out of breath when performing any of the techniques, stop what you are doing and rest.

- Do the techniques slowly and with control.

- Use the recommended products only in the manner they are demonstrated throughout the book.

- Never work directly on an acute injury.

- Start slowly. Progress at your own pace and gradually build on your successes.

- Be sure the environment in which you are performing the techniques is cleared of obstacles and that you have plenty of room to complete the techniques as they are suggested.

- Check in with your body each time you perform the techniques. Listen to your body and only perform the techniques that feel comfortable and right for your body at that moment.

- Do not roll the foam roller directly over joints, especially the knees.
- Do not place the Super Pinky Ball directly on your bony parts.
- Utilize and engage your core to support yourself through the techniques.
- When performing these techniques or any self-care, seek always a productive response in your body. Often this is described as the oxymoron of "hurts so good." It is a feeling of slight discomfort that at the same time feels productive and "good." If the sensation feels like pain, but without a "good" or productive aspect to it, your body may tighten up to protect itself because it feels a potential for injury. Muscles have receptors (called "muscle spindles") that monitor force applied to a muscle. If these receptors feel that the muscle is in danger of injury, the receptors send out a signal that will tighten up the muscle in order to protect it. So pushing through a technique is not beneficial and can be counter-productive to our goal of creating ease.
- Explore and enjoy the techniques. Consider this book an "idea" book. Try different pressures and angles and see what changes you can make through experimentation.
- Be gentle with yourself and have fun!

There are no mistakes.
The events we bring upon ourselves,
no matter how unpleasant,
are necessary in order to learn
what we need to learn;
whatever steps we take,
they're necessary to reach the
place we've chosen to go.

— *Richard Bach*

let’s get started

You hold in your hands possibility and potential.

If you allow it, this book can provide an opening; a new way of looking at yourself, your body, and how you connect with your life. Are you ready to connect with your body, your mind, and your spirit in new ways that support a healthy and joyful you?

With this book I am offering you a starting place—simple, quick, easy, and pleasurable techniques that can set you on your way to experiencing joy and ease again in your body. There is certainly much more information available to you than offered in this book, but my goal is to introduce you to a new way of being, not to overwhelm you. Think of this book as a starter kit, and I will share with you at the end of the book resources that can take you further on your journey towards optimal health and well-being, if that is where you want to go.

Let's begin right now with where you are. The equipment we will use is minimal and the techniques are simple. You can start today; all you need to do is show up. This book will be your guide for an expedition into a territory that most people have almost forgotten, a territory and landscape created by your cells and your being. This is an expedition of unlearning many concepts that we have unconsciously accepted about discomfort and pain in our bodies and remembering our true state of ease and luminosity. I would like to present another way to look at your amazing and most magnificent body.

Where We Are

The majority of Western society is currently entrenched in a medical paradigm that is not based on health and wellness, but on illness. This paradigm is not in alignment with our bodies, our minds or our spirits. People seeking medical help typically are treated as isolated components versus a whole, unique, complex, interwoven being. You may be one who is eager to discover ways to recover wholeness and vitality, and I am here to meet you wherever you are on this journey, whether it is at the beginning, somewhere in the middle, or further along your path.

Too often, pain in the body is normalized and accepted as a process of life and of aging. Or perhaps we entirely ignore signals of discomfort because we don't know how to make the pain go away, and we are not clear where to turn for help. Maybe on some level we're scared that the signals from our bodies might be indicative of serious problems, so we look away, not ready to address possible scary scenarios that might turn out to be real.

It's time to come out of hiding. I urge you to have the courage to rethink pain and confront it head on. Create space for the discomfort as a place for opportunity and learning. Open the closet door and look at all the monsters you imagine are hiding in the darkness. Turn on the light and shine it directly on your fears. Many times the monsters are just dust bunnies that our imagination and fears have pumped up, making them bigger than what they really are.

Pain in the body is not normal. It is a warning signal from your body that it is out of balance in some manner, and the imbalance needs to be investigated. As you progress through this book, please do not aggressively push through a technique if you feel non-therapeutic pain. We are not looking to have you force your body to do something that feels injurious and painful; your muscles will tighten up in order to protect your body from harm. That is counter-productive to the positive changes we are looking to create. You will learn to differentiate between pain that feels productive and therapeutic (that "hurts so good" feeling), and pain that feels injurious (a hurting feeling without the feeling of also being productive). We are looking to reconnect with the joy, flexibility, strength, and mobility that is your body's natural state.

Sometimes we think our body's natural state of being is that of always being in discomfort—please do not accept pain as something that is a natural course of life! Oftentimes we even accept pain as being the common path of bodies that are aging. Pain and discomfort are not an expected result of aging—old age is *not* a disease! How often do you hear people attribute an ache to "old age" and simply give in to all their symptoms? The aging process is not something which we are doomed to endure with uncomfortable, limited range of motion and stiffness. Many times stiffness and decrease of mobility as we age are due to lack of motion and an increase of restrictions in the soft tissue around our joints. Our natural state of being is that of ease, flexibility, and joy... right up until the day we take our last breath.

The Hidden Message in Our Bodies

For most of us, our bodies are desperately trying to get our attention. The signals at first are subtle, but these are often ignored in our quest to get things done and create a life of busyness, multi-tasking, and importance. When we don't listen to these subtle signals, the body must create a more urgent call to get our attention and this translates as discomfort and pain.

Let's face it—pain is unpleasant, whether its source be emotional or physical. Most of us recognize that physical traumas create a disruption in our physical bodies and usually create an emotional upset as well. Not as many people are aware that emotional and psychological traumas, at the time of trauma, create measurable disturbances in the physiological balance of our bodies. When ignored and pushed aside, trauma—both physical and emotional—becomes trapped in our bodies. For the purposes of this book, we will define trauma as experienced fear and pain, regardless of its source. Peter Levine, in his book *Waking the Tiger: Healing Trauma,* succinctly states, "Trauma is trauma, no matter what caused it."[1]

Trapped trauma in our bodies begins to impede the natural functioning of our cells. Without a release, the trauma becomes energetically lodged in our bodies, often traveling through the soft tissue. The restrictions of trapped trauma tighten us, creating inflammation and lack of ease. Certain movements that used to be effortless can become uncomfortable. We begin to avoid the activities that once gave us balance and joy. A daily walk or exercise can become pushed aside, and we start to forget how powerful and crucial moving is to our bodies.

Lack of movement creates restrictions—emotionally and physically—and begins a downward spiral of losing some of our natural ability of movement and ease.

Our bodies are by design created for movement—not excessive sitting and passive activities. The muscles pump the vessels of our immune system; movement keeps our joints lubricated, like the oil in our cars lubricates the parts and keeps them working optimally. Lack of movement creates restrictions—emotionally and physically—and begins a downward spiral of losing some of our natural ability of movement and ease.

Symptoms of pain can seem mysterious and appear to have no direct association with a remembered trauma. Pain can creep upon us, slowly, until one day we realize that we hurt. People are often mystified because they cannot remember a single event that triggered their pain. Sometimes there is clearly a defining trauma, like an accident or an operation. Many times, however, this is not the case, and people feel confused and stuck.

As time goes on, and as our discomfort continues without resolution, we may start to dissociate from our bodies. We think that this strategy of hiding our heads in the sand will help us somehow; if we ignore or try not to feel the pain or fear, it might eventually go away. But, for the most part, this process of avoidance, at best, just doesn't work. At worst, it creates a feeling of distrust within ourselves. Instead of connecting as a unified being—a team—we may look upon our bodies as adversaries and burdens. Before we know it, we may even direct anger and resentment towards our bodies. Meanwhile, our bodies are simply trying to heal and maintain balance, desperate to wake us up to our physical and emotional needs through the messages of pain.

What Do We Need?

You and your body need each other. You cannot physically be on this planet without your body. Just think about that for a moment... I see many people give more care and consideration to their cars than their own precious bodies. I believe, oftentimes, this neglect is due to lack of knowledge and fear. And that makes sense because we haven't been taught to trust or listen to our bodies. We have been taught to put our trust in being busy and productive, ignoring the messages our bodies send us, especially if these messages compete with our need to get more done in less time.

Because of what we've been taught, or not taught, we are not really sure how to help ourselves without drugs or massive amounts of medical treatments that don't seem to yield lasting, permanent results. Chasing after symptoms, we feel something is off. We intuitively know that we should be able to care for ourselves in a way that is comfortable and even pleasurable, but we haven't been given the training or tools to do so—until now.

This is your call to action. Move into the pain instead of avoiding it. Experience it. Go through it. Give yourself permission to feel. Allow yourself to let go. You are safe in this space that I am creating for you. I want to put you in touch with your inner knowing and wisdom. I want to help you stop compartmentalizing your being and heal. My greatest passion in life is to see people recover their connection to their bodies. Their inner luminosity will begin to shine forth again; a sparkle will twinkle behind their eyes as they return to ease.

Using Your Right Mind

In this book, we will use our brains in two ways to assist our healing: visualization and feeling. Very simply, the brain is divided into two lateral hemispheres that each exhibits different patterns of processing information for us: the right hemisphere and the left hemisphere. The left side of our brains controls our thinking processes; our rational, logical, linear ways of viewing and analyzing our experiences. Language occurs on the left side, as well as our concept of time. Our perception of our bodies as separate and unique from others occurs on this side, and we feel our bodies as solid.

This is your call to action. Move into the pain instead of avoiding it. Experience it. Go through it. Give yourself permission to feel. Allow yourself to let go.

The right side is our artistic, creative region, and this is where non-linear processing occurs. Instead of language, our right side processes information in pictures and collages. It is our feeling and sensing side. Not processing time, the right side processes all information as in the now. Here is where we are expansive and flow with all that is; our bodies feel fluid, and we experience oneness with all of life. The left side is where our non-stop internal chatter and judgments originate; the right side is where we experience peace, joy, and bliss.

The two hemispheres work together to provide us with a seamless perception of our reality; we do not consciously recognize which side of our brain is being utilized when we are processing information. It is an automatic function in a normal, healthy brain. However, much of our current, modern lifestyle utilizes more of our left hemisphere than the right. Work, school, our focus on time and lack of time, getting things done, analytical skills, to-do lists, worrying about the future and worrying about the past are all perceptions that are processed in the left side of our brains.

There is a wonderful autobiography written by Jill Bolte Taylor, entitled *My Stroke of Insight: A Brain Scientist's Personal Journey.* Jill shares her stunning story of a stroke that impeded the functioning of the left hemisphere of her brain. It took eight years of determination and tenacity to regain the functioning of her brain's left side.

She shares her life as lived with only the right side of her brain processing her daily experiences:

> To the right mind, no time exists other than the present moment, and each moment is vibrant with sensation. Life or death occurs in the present moment. The experience of joy happens in the present moment. Our perception and experience of connection with something that is greater than ourselves occurs in the present moment. To our right mind, the moment of now is timeless and abundant.[2]

Both sides are equally important to our ability to function and thrive on this planet. We are not looking to favor one hemisphere over another. Our left brain is critical in its function of diligently reminding us of the details of our life:

> Through the use of brain chatter, your left brain repeats over and over again the details of your life so you can remember them. It is the home of your ego center, which provides you with an internal awareness of what your name is, what your credentials are, and where you live. Without these cells performing their job, you would forget who you are and lose track of your life and your identity.[3]

Since a majority of the dealings in our life typically utilize more of our left brain, how do we access the right side and start to tap into healing and feelings of well-being?

We have a bridge between the two hemispheres called the corpus callosum. The corpus callosum is a thick layer of cells that carries information back and forth between the two lateral hemispheres. Our goal is to consciously experience a place of possibilities where healing can happen. We are looking to leave the judgments about what is or isn't possible (left brain), along with all the incessant internal chattering (left brain), and cross the bridge to our right hemisphere, reconnecting with our luminosity (right brain).

Crossing the Bridge

One method of crossing the bridge of the corpus callosum is by tuning into your emotions and feelings. Throughout the book I will ask you what you are feeling during a technique, what you may be sensing. We are not looking for logical, analytical thoughts (left brain) but emotions (right brain) like happy, sad, delighted, scared, relieved, etc. There are no wrong or right experiences as to what you may be feeling; just give yourself permission to let go and feel what rises to the surface, knowing that you are safe and can stop at any time.

Nature, beauty, and art can facilitate our travels to the right hemisphere. Since this part of our brain processes using visual images, art opens the gate of the bridge for us. The beautiful photography placed throughout the book will give you opportunities to let go of the left brain chatter and let yourself feel. Allow yourself to linger and soak up the healing that is available to us in nature and the wondrous beauty of these photographs.

John F. Barnes, PT has inspired and trained thousands of myofascial release therapists and written several books on healing. He is, himself, a master healer. John frequently utilizes a metaphor of turning a dial inside ourselves to change from one channel to another to help us find, and cross, that bridge between the hemispheres, reaching the place of release and remembrance of who we truly are. He calls the place of logic and reason (left brain) "Channel 5" and the place of our luminosity and essence (right brain) "Channel 3." John is always encouraging us to switch the internal dial and tune in to "Channel 3."

One summer, I was working with John at his Malvern, Pennsylvania, clinic for a week with three other visiting therapists at a Skill Enhancement Seminar. One of the therapists asked John why children and animals typically respond so quickly to myofascial release treatments. John commented that is because young children and animals haven't been taught anything to the contrary; they are usually in the limitless space of the right brain—the place of fantasies, dreaming, and possibilities. Our egos, limitations, and judgments are housed in our left brain, a place where children don't naturally linger. John continued to say that children and animals don't know that they can't heal, and so they heal.

Frequently, emotions are connected to a restriction. It is very common for people to experience emotions when releasing tight and restricted areas.

During our time of self-care, let's aim to set aside the limitations imposed upon us by our left brain and strive to open to the child-like experience of the beauty, freedom, and joy within each of us. It's still there if we peel away the hardened layers and really look underneath, rediscovering softness. Contrary to popular belief, being "tough and hard" doesn't make us stronger, it just keeps us, well, tough and hard. Softness keeps us pliable, flexible, and able to withstand the storms that come our way. There is strength and resilience in our ease and vulnerability.

How Do We Release Restrictions?

There are multiple ways to release your restrictions. Over the many years of my practice, I have observed the techniques that people have happily employed and joyfully returned to each day. I have selected the ones that are simple and effective and put them together for our use in this book. Play and have fun exploring. Observe what works for you and your body.

The most important concept in relation to healing is seeing yourself as an integrated, whole being, not isolated components. Because of this, I have not presented the techniques in categories to address specific aches and discomfort you may be feeling in your body. Let go and trust your ability to select a technique that is appropriate for you in the moment. All you need to do is dedicate a small amount of time each day to release your restrictions, and you will again begin to experience a flow and ease with your body and your life. Trust that working on your hips will help your shoulder. Working on your shoulders will help your jaw. Working on your feet will release your low back. Know that any work on releasing one part of your body has the potential to travel and release other parts. The fascial system literally connects your feet to your head and everything in between.

The fascia is a three-dimensional, spider-web-like connective tissue. It is made up of collagen and elastin fibers, with a gelatinous ground substance matrix. Fascia wraps around all your muscles, bones, organs, and each individual cell (of which we have over a trillion). A fascial restriction can have a tensile strength of up to 2,000 pounds of pressure per square inch. That means that fascial restrictions can pull bones out of alignment, impede the functioning of your organs and cells, and sometimes severely restrict the movement and ease of your body. Some anatomists believe that the fascia is more responsible for the movement of our bodies than our muscles.

What Does a Release Feel Like?

A release may be experienced in several ways. Sometimes people report a sensation of the restricted area melting, like butter, or lengthening, like taffy being pulled. Others may experience a pleasant warmth that spreads and travels. You may feel tingling, like circuits are opening. Perhaps it may even feel that your entire body has lengthened. Some people feel lighter and have a sense of coming back into their bodies. Maybe a release to you may feel like an internal spark has reignited.

Frequently, emotions are connected to a restriction. It is very common for people to experience emotions when releasing tight and restricted areas. Do not feel surprised if you suddenly feel like crying, yelling, moving, laughing or shaking; this is your body's way of releasing and discharging trapped emotional energy. Give yourself permission to let go and feel; healing occurs when we can let go. Know that you are safe in this moment. Allow yourself to let go of that which no longer serves the higher vision you hold of yourself.

How to Start?

I would suggest you start by looking through the photos in this book and see what catches your attention. Make a daily self-care commitment to yourself and your cells. Each day take 5-10 minutes to spend with your body and explore the different techniques in the book. Everyone can find 5-10 minutes each day. Once you start, you will probably want to spend even a little longer doing a couple of techniques in a session. People report back to me that they feel their bodies crave this practice; they actually look forward to and anticipate their self-care time. Patiently, and with self-compassion, listen. What is your body asking for on a particular day?

Another approach would be to sit quietly, with your eyes closed, while holding the book between your hands. Silently ask the question, "What do I need in this moment?" With your eyes still closed, open the book and see what presents itself to you. Alternately, you could hold the book, close your eyes, and silently ask for help with releasing a particular pain. For example, maybe your shoulder has been bothering you. You might silently ask, "Show me how to relieve my shoulder pain." With curiosity and an open heart, see what page you open to in the book.

Play and have fun exploring. Observe what works for you and your body. Let me know how your own creativity expands and any new ways you discover to utilize these techniques. Together we create a community, and it is by sharing that all of us benefit and grow. We all take turns being the teacher and the student, learning from each other.

How Will I Know I'm Making Progress?

John Barnes will tell people that "healing is not an event; it is a zig-zag journey." There can be that one, big "ah-ha!" moment and a symptom suddenly leaves us. Usually, though, our discomfort and unease have been traveling with us awhile, and it can take some time for them to release. As you practice and incorporate these techniques into your daily life, be observant for moments of ease where there were none before. You may find yourself going about your daily life and suddenly notice, "Oh, that used to hurt when I did that, and now it doesn't hurt any more." Or, "That person used to continually get under my skin, and now I don't react to them." Any glimpse of forward movement inspires hope that we are moving in the right direction, and that we are creating positive changes for ourselves and our cells.

This "zig-zag" journey of healing can mean that as one area releases, you may feel like there are new areas and sensation of discomfort that pop up. Returning to ease can be like peeling an onion; layer-by-layer we release restrictions and trauma. As the superficial layers are released, the deeper stuff that was buried now has an opportunity to be seen and freed.

You are cultivating a new awareness and connection with your body—your whole body—not just isolated components. Sometimes we direct our attention solely to the body parts that are sending the loudest messages of discomfort and dis-ease. Other areas may be restricted as well, but we may not be aware of those because their messages are more subdued. We tend to pay attention to the loudest messages. As these quiet down, we are able to hear other messages that have probably been there all along, but in the background. We just weren't paying attention; but now, with our new awareness, we can hear and feel the communication of our bodies.

Reconnecting With All of You

Exploring and releasing areas of restriction in your physical body leads you inward. We discussed earlier how both emotional and physical pain get trapped in the body. Physical self-care cannot help but release emotional trauma. The beauty of this is that we don't necessarily have to go through the experience of re-traumatizing ourselves by "labeling" and understanding the trauma. The energetic release that occurs will heal us on many, many different levels and layers.

These techniques are simple, yet powerful. They will open you to a new relationship with your cells; one that includes joy, health, courage, pleasure, freedom, trust, and ease.

Your newly remembered way of being will ripple out from you and touch everything and everyone with whom you come in contact. As you experience an increase of self-compassion, you will notice that you are kinder and more tolerant of others. Your joy will radiate out from you. You will begin to connect to a state of inner peace and well-being with your breath, going out in nature, using the foam roller, gentle movement and stretching, the little Super Pinky Ball, the inspirational quotes, and gazing at one of the spectacular nature photographs. The only person in our lives we can change is our own self. But, by changing ourselves—our cells—and creating ease within, we cannot help but create more peace and ease in the lives of those around us.

I truly believe with all my heart that life is supposed to be a joyful, wondrous, amazing experience for each of us. Sure, sadness and tragedy are also a part of the journey, but we have the power to choose whether to linger and wallow, or to experience and release the pain, come back again to the present moment, pull ourselves up, engage fully in our cells and rise again. A simple walk across the corpus callosum will take us to a place of inner peace and well-being, helping us to cope again and move out of the fog.

I have strived to make this book as beautiful as possible. My intent is that it will be a mirror for you; that the beauty of the book will reflect back your inner beauty and all the magnificence that is you. Please join me on a journey that has the potential to empower you, open you in unlimited ways, and return you to ease.

---

[1]Levine, P. (1997). *Waking the Tiger: Healing Trauma: The Innate Capacity to Transform Overwhelming Experiences* (p. 128). Berkeley, Calif.: North Atlantic Books.

[2]Taylor, J. (2008). *My Stroke of Insight: A Brain Scientist's Personal Journey* (p. 30). New York: Viking.

[3] Taylor, J. (2008). *My Stroke of Insight: A Brain Scientist's Personal Journey* (p. 32). New York: Viking.

Listen to your inner voice
for it is a deep and powerful source
of wisdom, beauty and truth,
ever flowing through you.
Learn to trust it,
trust your intuition,
and in good time,
answers to all you seek to know will come,
and the path will open before you.

— Caroline Joy Adams

let's get centered

My dad grew up on a small, self-sufficient farm in western Massachusetts.

When I was little, he would tell me stories about milking the cows and how it was always done on a three-legged stool. He patiently described to me how a three-legged stool is stable; it won't rock and the seat is always balanced. In order to experience balance and ease in our bodies, the legs of our milking stool—body, mind and spirit—need to be of similar length and strength. The connection and nurturing of all three is what creates a strong, balanced way of being: the seat of the milking stool.

To me, being centered is being present in the moment, feeling and trusting a wisdom that comes from deep within me. It is having all of me—my body, my mind, and my spirit—in balance and feeling an aliveness and empowerment from this balance. From this place of balance—my milking stool seat—life is full of joy and ease.

Please consider the techniques offered to you in this section just as important and relevant as the techniques included in the "Let's Get Moving" section of the book. These centering techniques offer opportunities of gently connecting again with yourself. As you become more comfortable with these techniques and utilize them daily, you will experience a renewed feeling of well-being, confidence, trust, ease and joy.

This above all,

to thine own self be true.

And it must follow,

as the night the day,

Thou canst not then

be false to any man.

— William Shakespeare

grounding

Grounding. That word gets tossed around a lot, but what exactly does it mean?

And how does it pertain to our connection with our bodies and our return to ease? I feel that grounding is our connection to the present moment through our bodies. By tuning in to immediate sensations experienced in our bodies, we are instantaneously engaged in the moment—this moment. Grounding enables us to cross the bridge—the corpus callosum—from our linear, ego processing left side of the brain to our feeling, sensing, in-the-moment side of the right brain. In doing this, we come back fully to our bodies.

There are multiple benefits to being grounded. "Grounded" people are typically experienced as calm, stable, "down to earth," and peaceful. Ungrounded people may appear to be distracted, forgetful, have a propensity towards being "hyped up," and emotionally charged. Oftentimes, people who are clumsy and accident prone are not fully present in their bodies. Devoting chunks of time thinking about the past or the future also can create feelings of despair or overwhelm. Grounding can stop that self-sabotaging inner dialogue loop and open us to peace, harmony, balance, and alignment. In fact, with grounding, your mind may become sharper, clearer and more focused. Without so much mental chattering, you will probably receive new insights and easily experience creative problem solving.

I know for me there have been plenty of times when I have not been fully present or grounded while driving or doing a chore. Because my mind was elsewhere, I lost track of what I was doing. I drove past the exit I wanted on the highway; I wasn't paying attention to my body while walking (because I was also on the phone and the timer on the stove was going off), and I banged my shin on a coffee table. Rushing, being fearful that something wouldn't get done, I have "accidentally" made messes that ended up taking more time to clean up than if I had slowed down and been present in the first place. All blatant reminders of when I am not grounded, and that I need an immediate course correction!

Luckily for us, there are many ways to become grounded, and each gives us flexibility and choices to reconnect with ourselves, returning to ease. I am providing you some suggestions for grounding; see what engages your curiosity, what feels right to you, and what is easy for you to do in the moment.

Touch the Ground

One of the easiest and quickest ways to ground is to walk barefoot in the grass. There is snow on the ground as I write this, so I realize this method is not always practical. When the weather permits, try it. The results can be an instantaneous feeling of well-being and release of stress. I love to lie on the grass and let go of my worries and pain. I lie directly on the grass, and feel myself sinking into the ground. I feel the support of the ground under me. Inside a building you can do a visualization of moving your awareness from the top of your head, down your body, through your feet and into the earth. You will notice that you suddenly feel supported, confident, capable, and very alive.

Go Outside

Take a walk outside without your phone or music. Walk for the experience of moving your body in a pleasurable way, not to maximize your workout or to push yourself. With each step feel your feet connecting and making contact with the earth. What does the air feel like on your face? What sounds do you hear? Can you distinguish between different bird songs and insects? I like to listen to the different textures of snow and dirt. My mother-in-law uses an expression that I just love, "Go outside and blow the stink off you!" Truly, going outside will "blow the stink" of negative thoughts and feelings off you and open you to the healing that can only happen in nature.

Grounding Stones

Some stones are known for their ability to facilitate grounding: hematite, smoky quartz, obsidian, red coral, and onyx are a few. You can carry a stone in your pocket and touch it when you feel that you need to ground, or wear jewelry that contains grounding stones.

Essential Oils

Essential oils can also help with grounding. There are many opinions on which oils are the best for grounding. It's all about what connects with you. For me, I like woodsy, earthy scents like cedar, sandal wood, and cypress.

Touch a Tree

Trees are very special to me and so wonderful in their gifts of helping us to ground and center. Touching a tree, and sitting under a tree, can instantly shift my mood and melt away any anxiety. If I cannot get outside, gazing upon a tree through a window can be just as effective.

Eat Some Root Vegetables

If you are feeling especially flighty and spacey, eating root vegetables can help to re-ground you. Beets, carrots, winter squashes, and potatoes reconnect us again with the ground. I start to ground just handling these vegetables. Scrubbing the dirt off them in preparation of cooking fills me with an appreciation and a connection to the earth. Cooking, in general, is also grounding, when you use whole, unprocessed foods. For myself, I also find that ginger root and Earl Gray tea settle me back into myself.

Take a Bath

Adding sea salt, Himalayan salt, Celtic salt, and Epsom salt to bath water can clear your head, center you, and ground you. My favorite is an Epsom salt/baking soda bath, shared with me by my friend, a holistic clinical nutritionist, Douglas Fleckman. Epsom salts can calm the central nervous system, reduce internal inflammation, reduce muscle soreness, and pull out heavy metals, such as mercury, that we absorb from our food and air. Our bodies tend to be on the acidic side, and the baking soda is alkalizing.

The recipe: Add one cup of Epsom salts and one cup of baking soda to your bath water. Soak 10-20 minutes and then shower. If you don't have a tub you can still reap the benefits by soaking your feet in a dishpan of warm water. Use 1/4 cup of Epsom salt and 1/4 cup of baking soda.

Feel free to make an event of your soak by burning a candle and adding some essential oils.

Tune in to Your Body

The body scan and diaphragmatic breathing techniques included in this section are very effective at grounding. Practice them as often as possible. Simple diaphragmatic breathing—something you do naturally—can be one of the easiest methods of starting a practice of grounding.

Play in the Dirt

Try gardening and working with the earth. Unplug from all of your electronics and have fun digging, weeding, potting, planting, and pruning. If you don't have access to the ground outside, try working with some potted plants.

An internet search will provide you with even more methods of grounding using sounds, yoga, and other movement modalities. There are no rules to any of this; experiment and discover what appeals to you. Explore, have fun, and play in the dirt.

We're so engaged in doing

things to achieve

purposes of outer value

that we forget the inner value,

the rapture that is associated

with being alive,

is what it is all about.

— *Joseph Campbell*

body scan

The purpose of a body scan is to bring your awareness into your body by reconnecting you to your body in the present moment.

This is accomplished through the feeling side of your right brain hemisphere. A body scan has the potential to not only promote body awareness and stress awareness, but also an experience of deep relaxation. It affords you an opportunity to tune in to different areas of your body without judgment or expectation. It is also a helpful technique when sleep may elude you or whenever your mind may be playing an endless loop of sad, angry, self-sabotaging or critical thoughts. Just experience the scan and see what you feel. Allow your body and the present moment to take over. You are taking a tour of your body and feeling what you sense in it today, at this moment, without any judgments or criticism. You may experience new insights and awareness each time you practice a body scan, for your body is dynamic and constantly changing. Each body scan I do for myself is a fresh experience and gifts me with new insights.

I like to begin the scan at my feet. Starting here allows energy to move down my body, and helps me to become more grounded. From our feet we then systematically move up our bodies, bringing attention to each main body part, making objective and compassionate observations—not judgments. You complete the scan of individual body parts at your head. Once you have scanned your individual parts, open your awareness to your body as a whole—not isolated components—seeing and scanning it as a complete, wondrous unit. Let any information you receive during the scan guide you as your focus on your active therapeutic techniques for that day. The more you practice the body scan, the faster you will be able to perform it. I now find I can quickly tune in to my body throughout my day. This helps me recognize how my body is responding to different stressors that I encounter, and I am able to release tension sooner.

When time permits, it is always fascinating to me to add a scan at the end of a self-care session as well as at the beginning. In this way, you will be able to monitor any progress in your body and track the effectiveness of your self-care efforts. Many people report to me that they notice a "before" and "after" in their bodies—the "beads" of their spines are now in alignment, ease where there was restriction, and it goes on. Amazing!

If you do not have the time to do a full scan after practicing some of the techniques, take a moment and just notice any changes in your body. Most of the time you will observe increased relaxation, but you may also notice more sensations as well—improved flexibility and posture, and feelings of well-being and peace, perhaps. This brief noticing sends a signal to your brain that positive changes were created, though perhaps subtle, and your brain will record these feelings. This makes it more likely for these sensations to stay with you and for you to want to continue practicing the techniques.

You can read through the guided body scan meditation first and use it as a basic outline for your journey. It's whatever works for you; my words may not lead you where you need to go, but they can be a starting place for you. Another option would be to record this guided meditation—or write one yourself—into a smart phone or another digital recording device while you are reading it aloud. Recording it will allow you to travel deeper into yourself without distraction. You may also visit my website and download a free audio of this mediation recorded with a background of soothing piano music: www.return2ease.com.

body scan meditation

We are going to begin by lying on the ground on a towel or mat. You are on your back, facing up. Give yourself a moment and completely settle in. Your legs are uncrossed, your arms are relaxed at your sides, and your eyes are closed. Lift up your shoulder blades and see if they will lie flat on the ground. Focus on your breathing, allowing your stomach to rise as you inhale and to release, or lower, as you exhale. We are going to let the mind take a little vacation as we focus our attention on what we feel instead of on what we think.

Now with your breath and awareness, travel down to your feet. Notice any sensations you may feel. You are simply making observations, like an explorer in a new territory, and noticing the environment without judgment. You are curious and objectively investigating this most interesting terrain. Where on each foot do you feel the ground? How is each foot positioned in relation to the other? How do your toes feel? How do the soles of each foot feel—separately and compared to each other? Can you distinguish one toe from another? Do you have any sensations of heat or cold? Where do you sense areas of ease or restriction? Do you feel any emotions connected with these areas?

Gently now and as you feel ready, using your breath and your awareness, travel up from your feet, noticing your ankles and lower legs. You are making objective observations of areas of tension and areas of ease. What does the space behind your knees feel like? Do you have any sensations of heat or cold? Do you feel any emotions connected with these areas?

When you are ready, move your attention up your legs, scanning your thighs as you reach the pelvic area. Are your hips resting equally and evenly beneath you? If not, what do you observe? What parts of the pelvic area are connecting with the ground? What sensations, or lack of sensations, do you experience here? How do your legs feel as they emerge from this area? Do you feel both of your legs are the same length, or do they feel different? What do you feel in the lower abdominal region? Do you feel any emotions connected with this area?

As you are ready, travel up to your chest. Using your breath and awareness, notice your ribs. Compare the right and left sides as you breathe in and breathe out. Take in a deep, deep breath. How far down into the lungs does your breath travel? Do you feel free or restricted in this area? Now exhale. What does the exhalation feel like? Travel along your spine and imagine it is a string of beads or pearls. Do all the beads or pearls line up, or do some travel to the right, or to the left? Are there emotions that float into your awareness?

Keep breathing and feeling. Notice your heart. Feel it beating. Do you feel any emotions as you explore this area? As you feel ready, travel to your shoulders. Are your shoulders resting equally on the ground beneath you? Notice objectively, any differences and any emotions you may feel with this area. Move your awareness down your arms, into your fingers. Are your arms the same length? Notice your wrists... your forearms... elbows... and upper arms. Do you have any sensations of heat or cold?

On your next breath, travel up your arms, past the shoulders, and arrive at your neck. How does this space between your head and shoulders feel? Does your head feel balanced or does it pull to one side? Are you noticing any sensations of heat or cold? Do you feel any emotions connected with this area?

As you feel ready, move your awareness along to your jaw. How is your tongue resting in your mouth? Are your teeth together, or apart? Notice your eyes... ears... and scalp... your chin, cheeks, and temples... the back of your head, and the top of your head. Can you feel your brain? Do you have any sensations of heat or cold? Do any emotions come to your attention?

When you feel ready, take one or two deeper breaths. Widen your focus, filling your whole body with awareness. Notice without judgment whatever is present. Sweep your attention from the top of your head to the bottom of your feet, experiencing your body as an entire unit. Listen for a moment to see if any new insights or awareness bubble up. What do you feel now about your body? Is it different from how you felt at the very beginning of this body scan?

When I was 5 years old,
my mom always told me that
happiness was the key to life.
When I went to school,
they asked me what
I wanted to be when I grew up.
I wrote down "happy."
They told me I didn't understand the assignment,
and I told them they didn't understand life.

— John Lennon

diaphragmatic breathing

You may be wondering why we might need instructions on how to breathe.

Just for a few moments, focus on your breath. As I asked you to do this, I noticed something in myself: I started focusing on my breath. I also noticed that my heart rate slowed slightly, and I felt a little more relaxed. I am guessing you might have felt something similar.

Breathing is something that we do quite naturally and can perform involuntarily or without any thought. One of the amazing aspects of breathing is that it is also a bodily function that we can consciously or voluntarily control. In fact, it is the only bodily function that can function *both* voluntarily and involuntarily. Breathing exercises can act as a bridge to those bodily functions we don't necessarily have control over including blood pressure, heart rate, digestion, elimination, and circulation.

Engaging Your Breath to Aid in Healing

Some cultures believe that the breath can connect us to our spiritual essence of being; the breath may be the link between the conscious and unconscious. Perhaps you have noticed with yourself that when your mind and body are balanced, your breathing is deep, even, and rhythmic. Now think about what happens when you are tense, angry or under stress. Your whole body constricts and tightens. Breathing can become erratic and strained under these circumstances. Chronic stress and distortions in our posture can lead to fascial and muscular restrictions across the chest, ribs, and abdominal area. (The "Let's Get Moving" section will help remove restrictions you might find here.) Tightness in the chest region can create shallow and quicker breathing patterns due to the lungs not having the freedom to fully expand.

This is a technique that can potentially slow your heart rate, lower blood pressure, and reduce and release tension by calming the central nervous system.

You can perform a quick experiment to see what type of breather you are in most circumstances. Place your right hand on your chest and your left hand on your stomach, or abdomen. As you breathe, notice which hand rises more. If your left hand rises more with the inhalation, you are a diaphragmatic, or abdominal, breather. If your right hand rises more, you are a chest breather.

Diaphragmatic breathing goes by many names; deep breathing, belly breathing, and abdominal breathing are some of the more common names. Diaphragmatic breathing is a fancy way of saying that you are breathing fully and engaging your diaphragm with every breath. Basically, it is a rhythmic practice of expansion and contraction, using controlled breathing. However, it is marked by the expansion of the abdominal area instead of the chest.

This is a technique that can potentially slow your heart rate, lower blood pressure, and reduce and release tension by calming the central nervous system. It will detox your body (your marvelous body is designed to release 70% of its toxins through ***breathing***), increase the clarity of your thinking, aid in pain reduction, strengthen your immune system, improve the quality of your blood, strengthen your lungs and help prevent respiratory illnesses, and even increase your stamina. It is very simple with practice, and as you do it, you will awaken one of your body's most effective self-healing devices—your breath. If I had to pick just one technique from this book that I would encourage you to perform every day, it would be diaphragmatic breathing.

The diaphragm is a large muscle that is horizontally located just beneath your ribs and above your stomach. When you take a deep abdominal breath, the diaphragm rises up, pressing against the lungs. Diaphragmatic breathing can renew your entire system for it uses the full capacity of your lungs, removing stale air and toxins.

Your breath truly integrates the mind, body, and spirit. You can consciously choose to perform this technique in times of tension, anxiety or anger. By controlling our breath, we can control our state of mind. Taking a few moments in your day to really pay attention to the inhalation and exhalation that supports your life will balance and clean your body. The inhalation brings in fresh air, fresh ideas, fresh thoughts, and fresh creativity. The exhale releases toxins, old habits, old thoughts, and old ways of being. Let each breath gift you with increased vitality and ease.

Instead of giving myself reasons why I can't, I give myself reasons why I can.

— Unknown

gratitude

This book is about the creation of ease in our bodies through simple, yet extremely powerful techniques.

For me, one of the most effective and powerful means to ease is the experience of gratitude. Like grounding, gratitude is a word you've probably heard tossed around a lot, but how can a word help to create ease in your body?

It doesn't. It's not the word gratitude, or just saying the words "thank you" that create ease. Gratitude is much, much more than an expression of thanks towards someone or something. The version of gratitude that carries healing potential and transformation is actually a feeling. It starts deep within your being, building into a wave that then moves into your heart space. From your heart this wave gains momentum and ripples out from you, affecting everyone and everything around you. If you allow it, this wave of feeling can then shift our mind and your entire being into an expansive, loving space.

Gratitude is not the same thing as positive thinking. You will feel more positive and upbeat as you begin your gratitude practice. Thinking, however, can be a method of rationalizing or explaining something. Positive thinking is something that happens more in the left side of the brain and doesn't necessarily bring with it a positive feeling. Positive thinking is also more superficial; gratitude penetrates our deepest being. The feeling is what we're going for here; we want to cross the bridge from our left thinking side over to the right side of our brain. Remember, this is where we heal, and we do that through feeling, not thinking. We want to leave the left thinking side and cross to the side where miracles and shifts occur.

The Feeling of Gratitude

Start by bringing to mind an experience that leaves you feeling joyful, content or peaceful. Take a minute and sort through the pictures in your mind. You're looking to retrieve the pleasant and happy memories of your life. The feeling we're looking for is created by your remembrance of an experience or a moment that is deeply moving for you. This will be different for each person.

What can instantly, literally put a smile on your face and light you up with a deep, heartfelt emotion? Is it the thought of a beloved pet? Your feet sinking in the sand at the beach as a breeze caresses your face? The time your teenager sought you out and said how much he or she loves you? A kindness a stranger extended to you without expecting anything in return? Bring your awareness to the present moment. How do the clothes feel on your body? Cozy? Warm? Soft? How did that steaming hot cup of tea or coffee feel in your hand this morning? How does natural beauty, such as a sunrise or sunset, make you feel?

Anything can bring on and activate feelings of gratitude if you allow it. The memory doesn't have to be something "big" or profound. Everyday joys count just as much as the big, once-in-a-lifetime moments. It can be the $20 you forgot you had in a jacket pocket and it was there as a surprise, just when you needed it. It could be a phone call from a beloved friend that brightened your day. Maybe it was that haircut that turned out just as you had hoped and you feel fabulous. A memory of gratitude can be anything as long as it puts a smile on your face and causes you a deep feeling of joy and happiness.

Once you have a memory, or a vision, that calls up any positive emotions—happiness, coziness, joy, laughter—hold that memory in your mind's eye for a moment. Close your eyes. Keep feeling and experiencing. Feel it deep in your belly. Keep feeling until you experience deep appreciation for this moment in your life. Keep feeling the joy and thankfulness, and at the same time, move your awareness into your heart space. Now hold that feeling of thankfulness in your heart. Sense that this feeling builds and starts to expand. It will feel as if it is expanding right out of you. You might start to feel yourself soften internally. Can you feel your cells come alive? Do you feel expansive? Do you feel a deep thankfulness? This is gratitude.

This feeling of gratitude can expand your consciousness and, with the shift in your heart space, instantaneously lift your spirits. Gratitude can change your life for the better in an instant. So simple and easy with beautiful, powerful results. Oftentimes gratitude takes us on a journey from where we are experiencing lack and fear, to a new place of having all we need, and being all we need, in this moment. We come back to ourselves feeling confidant, purposeful, abundant, and easy in our bodies.

Feelings of lack and feelings of fear contract us, creating restrictions. Remember that quick technique we just did a moment ago where you felt joy and gratitude? Now think of something that worries or scares you. What do you feel in your body? Just writing about it, I felt my jaw tighten, my hips grip, and my stomach clenched. Ugh. This is where disease happens. Now call up the memory you selected that triggers your feeling of gratitude. Ahhhhh... so much better. Did you feel a release and a softening? My body just released even more with an audible exhale. Okay, we're back on track after that little detour.

Everyday joys count just as much as the big, once-in-a-lifetime moments.

And that was just a little detour. Some days can seem like a total derailment of all you hold near and dear. Life brings the dark as well as the light, but know that we always have the choice of how we wish to experience it, and how to move through them. No one can ever take that away from you. Some things have to be faced and there is no way to get through them except to go through them. However, staying in a space where you lose all hope and everything seems dark perpetuates more of the same. It is during these times you will call forth your "go-to" memory that triggers the opening of your heart. Please know that in times of great despair and grief it is okay to gift yourself with the feeling of gratitude that lifts you up, that gives you hope and light.

Life brings the dark as well as the light, but know that we always have the choice of how we wish to experience it, and how to move through it.

Gratitude is more than "turn that frown upside down," but sometimes the physical act of smiling can create that shift when we're stuck. I know there have been times when I have been mad, stuck on some loop playing in my head, and my dear husband tried to get me to smile. Stubbornly, I worked to resist him and hang on to my anger. Finally giving in to his charm and persistence, I allowed myself to let go. I couldn't hold out any longer; it was taking more effort to remain stuck than to let go and soften. I smiled at him and immediately felt ease returning to my body. The physical act of smiling brought a lightness and new way of seeing. Suddenly, I was relaxed; the tension left my body. I couldn't even remember what it was that had upset me. Kevin will sometimes say to me and our kids, "Smile first thing upon waking, and your whole day will go better." It's true. Just try it.

Experiencing Daily Gratitude

Like any new habit we would like to make permanent, experiencing daily gratitude takes daily practice and commitment. Each day, aim to write down 1-3 things for which you can truly feel and experience gratitude; you can expand the list as you feel ready. If looking at a blank page seems difficult, there are options for journals that provide you with an easy format that you can follow each day. The one that I use is called *Daily Gratitude and Intention Journal: An Abundant Life* by my friend and colleague, Heather Doyle Fraser.

Some days will be easier than others. There will be days that seem like everything that could go haywire, does. In times like these, look at your day objectively and really get back to your basic needs. Did you have access to clean water today? The answer is probably yes. Many people around the world, however, don't have access to clean water or sanitation. How blessed I am that my toilet worked today and I had access to nutritious food. As I write this, it is winter and I am so very blessed to have a warm house to shelter me. I have access to electricity and trust the lights to go on when I flip a switch. Some people never experience this luxury.

Noticing all this I start to feel a sense of abundance, humility, and gratitude for my life. I begin to open and appreciate all that I have, instead of all that seems to be lacking. I become expansive and move out of the feeling of contraction. The shift may seem subtle, but it is a huge life changer when you practice day after day. Many times there are more blessings and abundance in our daily lives than we initially recognize. We just have to open our awareness and move through the feelings of lack and fear.

The Power of Gratitude

The practice of gratitude has the power to rewire your brain. As you acknowledge your gratitude and the power it has in your life, the more you will easily feel and experience it. After a time of this perspective shifting, you will more readily live in a space of abundance, rather than lack. Gratitude can change your life for the better; I have witnessed many lives completely transformed by this practice.

The active practice of gratitude can help you shift your perspective of events and people so that you have more compassion, tolerance, and patience. It's such a simple and easy technique with huge, powerful results. Oftentimes gratitude takes us on a journey from where we are experiencing lack and fear, to a new place of having all we need, and being all we need, in this moment.

Be who you are and

say what you feel,

because those who mind

don't matter,

and those who matter

won't mind.

— Dr. Seuss

let's get moving

Five to ten minutes a day of self-care has the potential to allow ease and mobility to return to your everyday life.

Of course, after five to ten minutes you may feel so good that you will actually want to continue longer—this is an amazing scenario! Remember, though, to start slowly and progress according to how your body is feeling and what it is telling you. Whenever you are practicing these techniques, it is better to do one technique thoroughly and patiently than to quickly rush through multiple techniques. Quality counts more here than quantity—a reverse of what we typically experience in our lives.

Sometimes in our quest to jump in head first with a new practice, we become discouraged when we don't see the results we want quickly and immediately. We are a society of immediate gratification. Remember, though, that you have had a lifetime of not practicing these techniques. As John Barnes frequently reminds us all, "Healing is not an event, but a journey." It may take a little while for your body to realize the result you are looking to achieve, but any forward movement, any positive change, is progress.

Five Minutes Is All You Need

So, how do you achieve that forward movement? All you really need is five minutes a day. That feels doable, right? Everyone can usually find five minutes in their day. At the same time, realize that whatever you were doing before wasn't working the way you desired, or you wouldn't have picked up this book. Einstein's definition of insanity is doing the same thing over and over again yet expecting different results. So break the cycle that isn't working for you, and take that different action. Now you have the tools and guidance to do something different for yourself.

For the best benefit, you will need to devote at least two minutes to release a restriction, sometimes longer. As you begin this practice, use the time of waiting as an opportunity to feel and sense; listen to and reconnect again with your body and your inner self. As I started to practice these techniques, I found that I needed to use a clock or timer. When I felt that I had held a ball on a restricted area for the minimum two minutes, I would glace at the time. How stunning that only 30 seconds had passed by—not two minutes! Most people experience the same time warp when starting these techniques, so at the beginning I suggest that you use a timer so that you can fully let go and experience the release. The timer has the responsibility for keeping you in position for the two minutes, not you. This will allow you to experience the full benefits of each technique for your entire body.

Where Do I Start with the Techniques?

This book was carefully crafted to invite you back to yourself, not create more rigidity or feelings of heaviness in your being. The intention behind it all is that you might tap into the beauty throughout the book to facilitate a shift into your feeling, sensing self, where you open to the possibilities of healing and ease.

As you explore the techniques and how your body responds to them, you may also wish to start looking through the photos and see what catches your attention. Each day gift yourself with 5-10 minutes as devoted time with your body and simply explore. Listen. What is your body asking for on a particular day? You might enjoy randomly opening to a page daily and focusing on a technique or an inspirational quote. As you start to become more comfortable "going within," you can tune in to your body, connect, see if you feel a "request," and then open the book. I am always amazed at the guidance and requests that come forth when I am willing to let go and listen.

When I am doing a longer self-care session and am able to incorporate multiple techniques, I like to use my foam roller before doing any Super Pinky Ball techniques.

For me, I find that the foam roller loosens up large groups of soft tissue. The Super Pinky Ball then easily goes deeper into the targeted area.

I use the gentle movement techniques throughout my day. They can be so much fun and feel playful! These gentle movements engage our bodies in the full range of motion of our joints. Any time my body has been in a prolonged, static position—working at the computer, standing, cooking, long car rides—my first go-to technique is one of gentle movements. A couple of leg swings, arm swings, a spinal twist, and I feel ease again.

Office workers have shared with me they have found discreet ways to incorporate the movement techniques during their day. Others, a bit more bold, have done them openly. In fact, one lady's office was curious as to what she was doing, and the entire group started to utilize the techniques! They now make regular breaks of the gentle movements, and I've heard they all smile more.

We want to remind our muscles each day how they are supposed to move so they don't forget and become shortened.

Our shoulders especially tend to exist in a little square box of isolated movement that does not utilize the full range of motion of this area. Most of us spend our days with our hands and forearms in front of us, our upper arms at our sides, typing at the computer, driving, cooking, and using our electronic devices. Then it is a reach up high on a shelf, or raking leaves, or some extended movement we ask of our shoulders and—ouch—our shoulders suddenly hurt. We want to remind our muscles each day how they are supposed to move so they don't forget and become shortened. Utilizing the gentle movements at least once a day can help preserve the range of motion in your joints, break up scar tissue, and keep your muscles at their proper resting length. This all creates ease and freedom in your body.

What Does a Release Feel Like?

What exactly are releases and what do they feel like? Release means to allow or, to enable something to enact freely. What would you feel like if you could be free from restriction? Reflect for a moment on the word "release." What do you feel in your body when you say this word? What comes up for you? Sometimes I feel an opening. Sometimes I feel that I have been freed from bondage. It can feel superficial; it can feel deep. Emotions that bubble up as trapped trauma can be freed and released.

A release can feel different to different people. Even in your own body you will start to notice a variety of sensations that you will intuit as a "release." Sometimes this can feel like a spreading warmth; other times it may feel like butter melting, or taffy being stretched. Some people have reported sensations of electrical charges suddenly traveling through their bodies, and others have shared that they feel a sense of lightness. There is no "one" way to experience a release of a restriction. You will intuitively know that a release has occurred. Trust your body.

Less Is More

I often am asked about using two or more balls at once. If one is good, more must be better, right? The answer to this is, less is more, not the reverse. Slow down; focus on one area. Our current society prizes multi-tasking, but this is not an area in which it would be of benefit. My own experience has been that using more than one ball at a time sends too much stimuli to my brain. For me, I cannot thoroughly process what is happening when I use more than one ball at a time, and the releases are not as complete. So my advice, at least with the techniques presented in this book, is to stick with one ball.

Correctly Engaging Your Core

Throughout the techniques I will ask you to "engage your core." Engaging your core—your trunk area/abdominal area—is a contraction, and the foundation of correct posture and movement. It is something that you can work towards becoming habitual, and use this technique when walking, driving, sitting, running, pulling, standing, lifting—just about all the time! An engaged core gives us greater stability with all of our daily movements.

Correctly contracting the core creates a cylinder of protection around your mid-section—all the way around your trunk, not just the front abdominal section. Engaging your core is not the same as sucking in your stomach. Sucking in your stomach will actually give you the opposite effect of destabilizing your core. A quick way to experience engaging your core is start to laugh or cough. You should feel your mid-section muscles tighten up and expand slightly outwards—the opposite of sucking in this area. It is not a pushing out, but more like a bracing. Initiating either of these actions during the day will help you practice engaging your core, and you will soon be able to do this without any thought.

Another way to engage your core is to pretend you are about to be punched in the stomach. Automatically we brace and protect ourselves by tightening up and widening our stance. (It is very easy to knock over someone standing with their feet close together, so widen your stance to give yourself a better base of support.) Your spine, neck, and head remain in a neutral, relaxed position.

You can always consult with a myofascial release therapist, therapeutic massage therapist, chiropractor, physical therapist, occupational therapist or personal trainer to see if you are doing this correctly.

Visual Reminders

In our family room we have a pretty ceramic bowl on our coffee table that houses an assortment of balls: a Super Pinky Ball, a baseball, a tennis ball, a golf ball, some soft four inch balls, and a lacrosse ball. And the rollers are vertically contained in a tall basket, also in the family room. It's been my experience that I need to have the rollers and balls out in the open and not hidden in a closet or drawer—out of sight, out of mind truly applies here! I rely on the daily visual reminders or soon I forget about these fabulous tools. Walking by the balls and rollers sends a gentle message—a whisper—that I need to take some time for self-care.

As mentioned in the "Let's Get Started" section, our bodies are not random, isolated parts, operating independently of each other. Because of this, there is not a presentation of body parts to target for specific pain conditions. It is my greatest wish that you begin to see yourself as an integrated, whole being. If you have the courage to listen and explore, you will reap amazing transformation in your body and your being.

Before You Get Moving

If you haven't already done so, please take some time to review the "Let's Get Prepared" section of the book. There are some important safety tips and guidelines to get you confidently and safely on your way to ease.

This is the exploration
that awaits you!
Not mapping stars and
studying nebula,
but charting the unknown
possibilities of existence.

— Leonard Nimoy

the foam roller

Many of my clients hug their foam rollers upon their initial purchase!

I hear from many that, after learning how to use their foam rollers, they look forward to and anticipate their time of self-care! How incredible is that?

Just about anyone who has sore muscles can benefit from utilizing a foam roller. A foam roller is typically a cylinder-shaped piece of molded foam. The choices of foam density are usually soft, medium, and hard. You may have noticed that there are many choices regarding the texture of the foam—smooth, wavy ridges, and staggered bumps are a few—and each provides a different experience.

I personally like to have on hand an assortment from which to choose so that I can achieve the most appropriate pressure for each area as I practice self-care. As you become more adept at this practice, you will be able to read your body and know what you need on any given day. Some areas are usually more tender and restricted than others and the use of a soft roller usually yields better results on these spots. Other areas may have a bigger muscle group and be more open to the pressure of a denser roller (for example, the gluteal region).

If I had to pick just one foam roller in which to invest as a beginner, it would be a soft one. You can work more areas of your body with a soft, smooth roller than with any of the other options previously mentioned. As you guide this wonderful device, you will be able to target areas of restriction and bring about a gentle release—all on your own. Remember, the "no pain, no gain" paradigm can cause more tension in our physical and emotional bodies instead of a state of release, and relaxation. We are seeking to create feelings of pleasure and release, with the ultimate goal of ease and mobility.

My current all-purpose roller of choice is the OPTP Soft PRO-ROLLER™. It is 36 inches long and a comfortable choice for both beginners and seasoned "rollers." You need to use your roller on a flat, firm surface; directly using it on a carpeted floor works just fine. If you are rolling on a wood floor you might like to do the techniques on a yoga mat placed on the floor. Your clothing should be comfortable and not too loose; I've caught many a loose shirt under a roller—the same goes for long hair! Bare feet work best, but you can also wear socks that have grips on the bottoms.

Restricted muscles and fascia are not fully hydrated. As the restrictions are released, the tissues are then able to absorb water and nutrients again. Please consider drinking water after rolling; many people report that they become thirsty when using the foam roller. Have you ever put some dried fruit in a bowl and then slightly covered the fruit with water? After awhile, the fruit absorbs the water and becomes soft again. This is what happens to your soft tissues when you foam roll, so please make sure to drink extra water.

Foam rolling is best performed slowly and carefully; there is often a tendency to roll too fast. Remember, you are exploring as you roll, taking objective mental notes of tender or restricted areas. (These might be areas you would like to go back to and release with the Super Pinky Ball.) Using your body, you direct the roller, slowly, up and down over a targeted area. Then, if you desire, direct the roller back over those spots, holding the roller on a restriction. It can take a lot of core strength to hold the roller on a restricted area for an extended time. A couple of seconds for a hold is just fine; feel free to hold longer. Remember to listen to your body.

That is pretty much all you need. Remember not to roll directly over joints—especially the knees—or any recently injured areas or areas that are swollen. And anyone with osteopenia, osteoporosis or osteoarthritis should seek out a doctor's advice before rolling. Playfully explore with your foam roller, and you may also end up looking forward to using it at the end of your day!

shins release

(anterior lower leg release)

Photo 1

Photo 2

Photo 3

A great release even if you're not a runner!

- Place yourself in a tabletop position with the roller perpendicular to your body—just below both kneecaps—with your shins resting on the roller *(Photo 1).*
- Engage your core and pull your knees towards your chest, slowly rolling over your shins *(Photo 2).*
- When the roller reaches your ankles, begin to roll up towards your chest, still rolling over your shins. Do not roll over your knees *(Photo 3).*
- Slowly explore with the roller and see if you feel any restrictions. If you are able, pause on any restricted areas and wait for a release.

hip flexor release

(psoas release)

Photo 1

Photo 2

Photo 3

You can hold this position a longer length of time without putting a strain on your body. Try holding it for 2-5 minutes to experience a complete release.

- Lie on the floor, face down, with the roller placed perpendicularly across your lower abdominal area, just above your hip bones. (If this feels uncomfortable try moving the roller down closer to your hip bones.)
- Place your arms where they feel comfortable; you can rest your head on your hands *(Photo 1)*, tuck your arms under you *(Photo 2)*, or lay your arms out to the side *(Photo 3)*.
- Slowly let yourself sink into the roller.

This area can hold a lot of emotion. Know that you are safe and allow yourself to feel. Relax... breathe... soften... and let yourself go...

outside thigh release

(iliotibial band and tensor fasciae latae release)

Photo 1

Photo 2

Photo 3

Your soft roller is a perfect choice for this frequently tender area.

- Sit on the roller so that the roller is perpendicular beneath you *(Photo 1).*
- Shift onto the right side of your body and position your right buttock/hip region on top of the roller. Bend your right arm into a 90° position and, leaning forward, rest your right forearm on the floor *(Photo 2).*
- Your left arm will come in front of your chest, with your fingers resting on the floor. The left leg is bent, crossing over the right side of your body, with your left foot flat on the floor in front of your body *(Photo 2).*
- The right leg should be in a straight line with your hips, waist, shoulders, and head.
- Engage your core and use the power from your right arm, left leg, and core to roll up and down on the roller—slowly—staying within the hip region and exploring for areas of restriction *(Photo 2).*
- Make sure you don't roll over the right knee; keep the roller above the knee. If you can, hold any restricted areas for a couple of seconds.
- Repeat on the left side.

For a Deeper Release:

- Place your leg that is facing the ceiling on top of the leg on the roller and roll with both legs together—like a sideways plank *(Photo 3).*
- Make sure you have your core engaged.

low back release

(lumbar release)

Photo 1

Photo 2

Photo 3

Easy does it here. This region can be tender so aim to be attentive and patient.

- Sit on the floor with the roller perpendicular across your low back, touching the top of your buttocks *(Photo 1)*.
- Your knees are bent, with your feet flat on the floor *(Photo 1)*.
- Your arms are behind your back, supporting the weight of your upper torso. Your hands can be flat on the floor *(Photo 1)*. Engage your core, and, with your arms and legs, lift your torso up onto the roller *(Photo 2)*.
- Your arms will be straight, keeping your head and shoulders lifted up off the ground.
- If you feel any tension in your wrists, you can make a fist with your hands to keep your wrists in a straight alignment, your knuckles touching the floor.
- Slowly roll searching for areas of restriction. When you are aware of a restriction, pause and hold the roller on that spot for a couple of seconds.
- You can continue this technique into the buttock region.

front thigh release

(quadriceps release)

Photo 1

Photo 2

An area that is sometimes neglected and taken for granted... We rely on this area for its strength and stability.

- Lie on the floor face down with the front of your thighs—your quadriceps—on the roller *(Photo 1)*.
- Bend your arms so that your forearms rest comfortably on the floor *(Photo 1)*.
- Using your core, lift your shoulders off the ground *(Photo 2)*.
- Engage your core and roll up and down over your quadriceps.
- Slowly move on the roller being careful not to travel over the knees *(Photo 2)*.
- Search for areas of restriction, and if you can, hold for a couple of seconds.

neck release

(posterior cervical release)

Photo 1

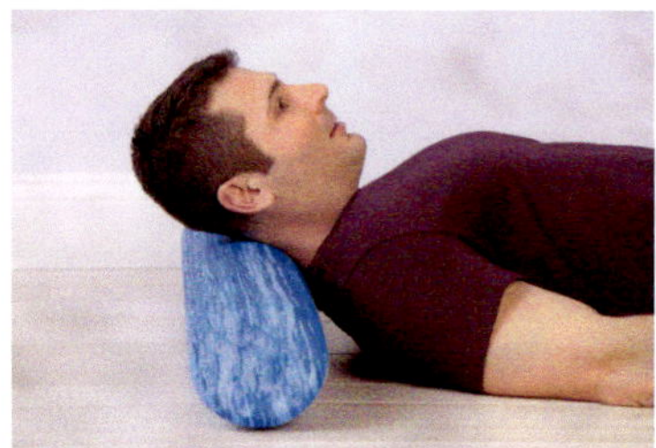

Photo 2

Make sure to do this technique slowly and with control. A couple of times of "nodding" will begin to release this area.

- Lie comfortably on your back.
- Place the roller under the curve of your neck. Gently let your neck sink into the roller *(Photo 1)*.
- Soften. Slowly, and without much pressure into the roller, roll your head left to right.
- You can stop at places that feel tight and hold for a couple of seconds to a few minutes, waiting for the area to soften and melt.
- When you are complete with that technique, try moving your head up and down as if nodding "yes." Bring your chin slowly to your chest *(Photo 2)* and then lift your chin towards the ceiling, extending the back of your head over the roller towards the floor again.
- Feel free to stop at any places that feel restricted and hold for a few seconds to a couple of minutes, waiting for the area to soften and melt.

shoulder blade release

(posterior scapula release)

Photo 1

Photo 2

Make sure you keep your elbows out to the side—parallel to the floor—not next to your ears; otherwise you might strain your neck.

- Sit on the floor with the roller behind you *(Photo 1)*.
- Place your hands behind your head, at the base of your head; elbows are out to the side. Knees are bent with your feet flat on the floor *(Photo 1)*.
- Lean back onto the roller so the bottom of your shoulder blades touch the roller. You may need to reposition slightly so you can ease your shoulders onto the roller *(Photo 2)*.
- Bend your legs; lift your pelvis and engage your core *(Photo 2)*.
- Now slowly roll up and down over the shoulder blade region, stopping at the base of your neck.
- Explore for areas of restriction. Stop and hold for a couple of seconds on any sore, tight places that you find.
- You can play with the angle of motion by turning your upper body slightly to the side so one shoulder blade has more direct pressure on the roller.

chest opener with spinal release

(anterior chest and spinal attachments release)

I find this technique to be very relaxing and calming. You can hold this technique for quite some time on the roller, for your neck and spine are gently supported. It feels so wonderful!

- Lie on the roller so it is aligned against your spine. Your head and neck should be completely supported on the roller.
- Let your arms fall open to a gentle "T" position, and feel a slight stretch across your chest.
- Hold this pose and enjoy the sensation of your body softening. Give yourself permission, for this moment, to let go and feel safe. Breathe. Feel and enjoy the connection to your body.
- You can gently roll back and forth over your spine. You are not rolling the entire width of your back, just slightly rolling/rocking to either side of your spine.

buttock release

(gluteal/piriformis release)

Photo 1

Photo 2

Photo 3

The largest muscle in our body is located here and it can hold tension and restrictions.

- Sit on the roller so that it is perpendicular to your spine *(Photo 1)*.
- Shift onto the right side of your body, and position your right gluteal region/hip region on top of the roller *(Photo 1)*.
- Place your left hand on the floor in front of your body *(Photo 2)*.
- Bend your right arm into a 90° position and rest your right forearm on the floor. Your left arm will be out in front of your chest, with fingers resting on the floor *(Photo 2)*.
- The left leg is bent, crossing over in front of your body, with the left foot flat on the floor in front of your body *(Photo 3)*.
- Engage your core and use your right arm and left leg to roll up and down on the roller, exploring for restrictions.
- If you can, hold any areas of restriction for a couple of seconds.
- Repeat on the left side.

Not everything that is

faced can be changed,

but nothing can be

changed until it is faced.

— James Baldwin

the super pinky ball

The Super Pinky Ball, in my opinion, is a cross between a tennis ball and a lacrosse ball.

For most people, it seems to be the perfect density for soft tissue releases. Portable and easy to use, it will quickly become one of your favorite self-care tools. Many people keep one at their work desk, in their car, and in their family room. It easily slips into a suitcase and goes with me on any trip away from home.

The key to using the Super Pinky Ball is patience. Now, some of you will say that you don't have patience, but maybe the reward for your patience hasn't been great enough—until now. A few minutes a day and you can access the mobility and ease that you thought would never return to your body. Doesn't that sound like a good trade-off? Give these techniques a chance and you will be amazed at your inner and outer transformation. It may even ripple out into other areas of your life. Perhaps one day you will observe yourself being more patient with another person or notice the chatter in your head—that little inner critic—is kinder than it once was.

For self-care using the Super Pinky Ball, place the ball in a spot of tenderness or restriction and wait. That's it. You're not going to roll, massage or try to "dig" out a restriction; you are just going to wait 2-5 minutes for a release. When beginning it is useful to use a timer; 30 seconds can seem like two minutes. A timer allows you the space to let go and not think about how long the ball has been in a tender spot. I like to start with two minutes, knowing that I can always hold a release longer if I so choose. The following techniques will give you a starting place, but experiment and discover what works best for you. Just stay off of bony parts and do not use the ball directly on your neck.

As with the foam rollers, there will be times when something softer is what your body needs for a release, and there will times when a release calls for something harder. Because of that, our family keeps an assortment of small balls in a beautiful ceramic bowl on the family room coffee table. There's a tennis ball, golf ball, Super Pinky Ball, lacrosse ball, baseball, and some larger, soft four-inch balls. This assortment gives us options.

If you are very tender, or suffer from fibromyalgia, you may wish to start with a soft four-inch ball. The four-inch ball disperses the pressure and is not as direct as the Super Pinky Ball. You can substitute another ball for any of the techniques in this section.

Self-care is all about listening to YOU and what is appropriate in the moment. Stay flexible and open when tuning in; your body's needs might change day-to-day—this is expected and normal. Your body is a dynamic living organism, not a static, mechanical machine. Trust yourself to listen and feel what your body needs in any particular moment.

foot roll

(plantar fascia release)

Photo 1

Photo 2

I highly recommend that you take the time to roll both feet, rather than just one foot, or you may feel unbalanced in your body.

- Stand in your bare feet next to a counter, a wall, or the back of a chair. This will provide you some balance support, should you need it.
- Completely roll the bottom of each foot on the ball for 2-5 minutes, making sure to roll your heel, the arch of your foot, the outside edges and your toes *(Photos 1 and 2)*.
- Engage your core while you are rolling on the ball.
- Feel free to pause the ball if you find a tender or restricted area and hold this spot until you feel a release.
- This is a great opportunity to also work on your balance at the same time you are rolling each foot.

shoulder blade release

(posterior shoulder release)

Photo 1

Photo 2

Photo 3

Keeping your knees bent and your feet flat on the floor can help take any pressure off your lower back.

- Lie on the floor, on your back, with the ball near enough to easily reach. Feel your body settle into the floor. Take a deep breath and slowly release it.
- Using your legs and hips, slightly roll your body to your right side *(Photo 1)*.
- Slightly lift up your left shoulder, and place the ball in the soft tissue around your shoulder blade *(Photo 2)*. Be careful to stay off your spine and also the actual bone of the shoulder blade. Gently sink onto the ball, allowing gravity to pull you in.
- Let yourself soften and let go. Keep the ball in this spot for 2-5 minutes.
- During the 2-5 minutes, check in with your body. Are you holding your breath? If so, please breathe. Scan to see if you are holding tension in your legs or any other place in your body. This simple act of awareness is like a magic wand; you'll notice an immediate release of tension just bringing awareness to your different body parts.
- Allow yourself to feel. Do you notice any feelings come into your awareness as you soften and let go?

shoulder blade release

(continued)

Here is another option once you have achieved a release in one spot, or if you still feel restricted in your shoulder area.

- Without moving the ball from the previous position above, play with moving your arm that is on the same side of your body as the shoulder the ball is under *(Photo 3)*. You will probably find another restriction. It's like making a snow angel: without repositioning the ball just drag your arm along the floor until you feel another area of tightness.
- Keep the arm in this new position and wait 2-5 minutes for a release.
- Be patient... Soften... And melt...

front shoulder opener

(anterior chest/pectoral release)

Photo 1

Photo 2

People are often surprised that they have sensations of tenderness and restrictions in this area.

- Stand with the front of your body facing a wall or closed door.
- Place the ball against the top of your left arm, on the front of your body. The ball should be just below the clavicle (collar bone), where your arm and chest seem to meet. Turn your head to the left, resting your head on the wall *(Photo 1)*.
- Now lean into the wall, pressing your weight against the ball. Feel free to move the ball to discover any spots that are restricted or tender. Try clasping your wrists behind your back for more direct pressure *(Photo 2)*.
- You can shift your position slightly with your feet and hips to also vary the pressure.
- Hold the ball on the targeted area for 2-5 minutes, using the time as an opportunity to observe your breath and objectively notice any feelings.
- Repeat on the right side.

buttock release

(gluteal and piriformis deep tissue release)

Photo 1

Photo 2

Photo 3

I find most people do not realize the tension and restrictions they hold in this area. For myself, I notice I tense this region when driving the car and need to work to consciously release the gripping sensation. If you are feeling rigid in your thoughts and feelings, this is a good place to start to create ease. There are three different options from which to pick for this release. One option is not better than another, but each will elicit different sensations and experiences as you release this area.

Option One: Release Using a Chair

- Lie on the floor, positioned in front of a chair (kitchen or dining room chairs are usually good choices), the ball easily within reach.
- Place both of your calves on the seat of the chair and scoot your buttocks closer to the chair. The position should feel comfortable and not put a strain on your body *(Photo 1).*
- Using your legs, lift up your hips. Pick either the left or right side and place the ball on the floor, estimating where your bum will land on the ball *(Photo 2).*
- Slowly, using your legs, lower onto the ball. There is no exact or even incorrect placement of the ball, except to stay off the bony part—the sacrum. You are looking to place the ball in an area that feels tender or restricted. There could be several, but know that you can come back to other spots at a later time. Feel free to move the ball until you find a tender spot *(Photo 3).* Once you locate a tender spot, stop moving the ball and hold the ball still.
- This area might be very tender, so be patient and wait for the tissue to soften and melt. Lowering all of your weight in one move might be too much pressure all at

buttock release

(continued)

once. I often find I need to "ease" into this area. You can use your legs to slowly lower yourself onto the ball as you are ready to receive more pressure.

- You will start to feel your gluteal region melting around the ball. Hold this position for 2-5 minutes. Keep softening and relaxing into the move, including softening your legs and your shoulders. Notice if you are holding your breath. If so, remind yourself to breathe. Give yourself permission to let go. Allow yourself to feel. What emotions or insights bubble up as you feel into the release?
- If time permits, switch sides.

Play with this release. You can use your legs for leverage, and gently roll more of your hip region onto the ball. Gently move on the ball until you find an area of discomfort and hold that position for 2-5 minutes.

Option Two: Release Using the Floor

This is like Option One, except you lie with your back flat on the floor, and do not rest your lower legs on a chair.

- Let's start with your right hip. Roll slightly to your left side so your right hip lifts slightly off the floor.
- Place the ball on the floor, estimating where your right gluteal region will land on the ball.
- Slowly, ease onto the ball. There is not exact or even incorrect placement of the ball, except to stay off the sacrum. You are looking to place the ball in an area that feels tender or restricted. There could be several, but know that you can come back to other spots at a later time. Feel free to move the ball until you find a restricted area. Hold the ball in this spot for 2-5 minutes.
- You can bend your right knee, or try extending your right leg so it lays flat on the floor.
- Let yourself go, relaxing into the melting and releasing. What are you feeling as this area releases?
- If time permits, switch sides.

buttock release

(continued)

Option Three: Release Using a Wall or Door

This option is more active than the other two versions, and a handy version to use at the office.

- Stand and lean against a wall or a closed door. Check to make sure the back of your head is touching the wall. This keeps your neck in a neutral position so that you are not thrusting your head forward.
- Now place the ball in either your right or left gluteal region. Using the strong muscles of your quadriceps, press onto the ball. Hold for 2-5 minutes and wait for the melting.
- If time permits, switch sides.

The most difficult thing

is the decision to act;

the rest is mere tenacity.

The fears are paper tigers.

You can do anything

you decide to do.

You can act to change

and control your life;

and the procedure, the process,

is its own reward.

— *Amelia Earhart*

movements & stretches

Stretching and gentle movements can make a significant difference in your body's day to day ease.

A stretch should feel good and create ease. If you feel pain stretching, whether with the static stretches or moving stretches—stop! Don't force yourself into a stretch or try to push past the point where you feel resistance. If you do, you are potentially creating the opposite effect—tightening your body further rather than releasing it.

Start Slowly

Work with non-moving stretches in this way: position yourself in the stretch until you feel the end of available motion. Stop at this point. Now, using your awareness, feel your body elongating, or lengthening, into the stretch. This is a process of naturally unraveling restrictions and *allowing* them to release instead of forcing a lengthening.

As you start to feel a lengthening, or elongating, you can now gently work the stretch a little deeper to the next point of restriction and hold. The holding is active. You are continuing to visualize the area being stretched as telescoping and elongating. As with the previous techniques, use the waiting time to make sure you aren't holding your breath and that you are softening all of you, not just the area being stretched. Like the ball techniques, aim to hold a non-moving stretch 2-5 minutes, never pushing past the point where you feel resistance. If you have recently had any joint replacement type surgery, please only use the techniques that have been cleared by your doctor.

Easy Does It

With the moving stretches, just let your body move naturally and in a pleasurable manner. The moving stretches are gentle and meant to be done with control. As with the non-moving stretches, don't push past the point of resistance. The moving stretches are not timed, as are some of the other releases in the book. They are easy to do and will help you experience ease throughout your day. I find if the thought of doing a technique pops into my head, I will follow through and do that particular technique. For me, I feel it is my body's inner wisdom communicating to me on what it needs in a particular moment.

For me, I feel it is my body's inner wisdom communicating to me on what it needs in a particular moment.

With all of these movements, you will need to continue to be aware of, and tuned in to, your body. Use your new skills of breath and scanning to stay present and listening. Feel... Breathe...Release...Enjoy.

windmills

Photo 1

Photo 2

Always start slowly with shoulder movement. You want to make sure your shoulders are warmed up—and movement is easy—before you increase intensity or add on more movement. This technique can even help to break up scar tissue in the shoulder region. A couple of sets of this technique are probably all you need at one time.

- Stand with your feet comfortably apart. Settle in. Feel your connection to the ground.
- Once you feel established with your connection to the ground, pull that feeling up through your body. Start by pulling it up through your legs, through your torso, and up through the top of your head. *(Photo 1).*
- Making sure you have lots of space around you, start to make windmills—circles—with your arms. It's a gentle movement of moving first one arm in a full circle, then the other—or whatever you can comfortably do—across the front of your body, alternating arms. *(Photo 2).*
- Play with making windmills in front of your body and at the side of your body.

Please listen to your body. Stop if you experience any pain in your shoulders doing this technique.

cat and cow poses

Photo 1

Photo 2

I enjoy the feel and natural flow of my body as I move between these two poses. A couple of sets will help to create ease in your body.

Cat

- Place yourself in tabletop position on the floor.
- Slowly, simultaneously, pull up from the shoulders and the hips, keeping your hands and legs connected to the ground.
- Your back will arch—like an upset cat—and your head will hang down towards the floor. Breathe into your back *(Photo 1)*.
- As you are ready, move into Cow pose.

Cow

- Start to release your stomach and your back. Let them soften, maintaining your strength in your shoulders and hips.
- Allow your stomach to gravitate towards the floor. Sense yourself pulling up from the hips towards the ceiling.
- Let your head travel up so you are looking out in front of you *(Photo 2)*.
- You can keep your eyes open or closed.
- Soften your abdominal area... Breathe... Soften...

child's pose

Photo 1

Photo 2

Another great technique for calming the central nervous system and releasing stress. You can hold this pose as long as you like.

- Place your body into a tabletop position.
- Keeping your knees and hand in contact with the floor, move your feet towards the middle of your body so that the inside edges of your feet are touching *(Photo 1).*
- Now, slowly, push with your arms so that your torso starts to move towards your feet *(Photo 2).*
- Your buttocks will start to lower to the floor, towards your feet. Your forehead and shoulders will start to drop towards the floor. Only push yourself back towards your heels as far as is comfortable for you *(Photo 2).*
- When you are at the place you'd like to stop, relax your arms, breathe into your back and let yourself go... All the way... Let it all go...

alphabet balance

Photo 1

Photo 2

Balance work produces almost instantaneous results in the body. Improving our physical balance also helps to keep our minds and spirit balanced. As you do this technique, notice any differences between your right and left sides. Do you receive any messages as to where you may be "off-balance" in your life?

- Stand next to a chair or a wall.
- Stand with your feet comfortably apart. Settle in. Feel your connection to the ground.
- Once you feel established with your connection to the ground, pull that feeling up through your body. Start by pulling it up through your legs, through your torso, and up through the top of your head.
- With your eyes, find a spot on the ground, about 10 inches out in front of you. Or, find a spot on the wall. You are going to stare at this spot as you balance
- Now, bending your right knee, raise your right foot off the floor and hold it in the air. Your foot should be about 12 inches off the floor (or as high as you can hold it if 12 inches is too much) *(Photo 1)*.
- You can use the chair for balance support; try letting go once you've regained your balance *(Photo 2)*.
- Picking upper case or lower case letters, "draw" the alphabet with your right foot in the air. The big toe will feel like the point of a pen, and the rest of the foot will follow.
- Repeat with your left foot

hanging low back release

This technique can help to calm your central nervous system and release anxiety. You can hold this pose for the length of time that feels comfortable to you.

- Stand with your feet hip width apart.
- Grab each elbow with the opposite hand.
- Bend forward, softening the knees. The bend is very gentle.
- Work with gravity and just hang. And soften.
- You don't have to do anything except breathe... and let go...

figure 8 hip opener

Photo 1

Photo 2

Many people report that their hips feel much more open and free after a few, short completions of this technique on each hip. This technique can even help to break up scar tissue in the hip joint.

- Stand so that the right side of your body is perpendicular to the back of a chair, a counter or a wall *(Photo 1)*.
- With your weight on your left leg, bend your right knee (next to the chair/counter/wall), and then use your bent knee to "draw" a sideways figure 8—or infinity sign—in front of your body *(Photo 2)*.
- The idea is to feel an opening in your hip that feels pleasurable and comfortable to you. Don't worry about perfectly making a figure 8. Usually making a couple of these feels complete, but listen to your own body.
- After completing the right side, change position so your left leg is next to the chair/counter/wall. Repeat the movement with your left leg.
- Note any difference from side to side.

swinging hip opener

Photo 1

Photo 2

Have fun with this! For me it taps into the joy and freedom I felt as a child swinging on a playground.

- Stand facing a counter, a wall or the back of a chair. (This is so you will have support with your balance should you need it.)
- With your weight on your left leg, swing your right leg across the front of your body, in a back and forth motion *(Photos 1 and 2).*
- Swing your leg only as far as is comfortable to you. You may notice that your range of motion increases after a couple of swings.
- Repeat with swinging your left leg.
- Take note of how each side feels. Sometimes there are differences in the range of motion and freedom from side to side.

spinal twist

Photo 1

Photo 2

Ease and mobility require a flexible spinal column. Some people report that they can even breathe more freely after a couple of these twists!

- Stand with your feet comfortably apart, and feel your feet firmly connecting with the ground. Settle in.
- Once you feel established with your connection to the ground, pull that feeling up through your body and up through the top of your head.
- Slightly let your knees have a soft bend in them and place your hands on the top of your shoulders. Place your right hand on your right shoulder, and your left hand on your left shoulder *(Photo 1).*
- Your elbows should stick out to the side, away from your body.
- Making sure you have lots of free space around you, engage your core and slowly start to twist your torso from right to left, and then left to right *(Photo 2).*
- Don't push the twists. Listen to your body.
- Focus on keeping your hips and legs rooted down, minimizing movement in your hips. You are moving from your waist, not your hips.
- You will naturally halt the motion when you feel ready to stop.

Never apologize for showing feeling.

When you do so,

you apologize for truth.

— Benjamin Disraeli

let's expand your skills

myofascial release

John Barnes's website and therapist locator: www.myofascialrelease.com

This is a wonderful resource for learning more about the John Barnes' Myofascial Release Approach®. The site also has an easy to use therapist locator section organized by geographical location.

Barnes, John F. *Healing Ancient Wounds: The Renegade's Wisdom.* Paoli, Pa.: Rehabilitation Services, 2000. Print.

A great book that uses anecdotes and stories to explore the healing potential of myofascial release. John shares his personal journey as well as stories from other therapists and patients.

Patterson, Joyce Karnis. *Comprehensive Myofascial Self Treatment: Your Path to Authentic Healing & Pain Relief.* Joyce Patterson, 2009. Print.

This book truly is comprehensive and offers myriad self-care techniques.

Stedronsky, Jill, and Brenda Pardy. *Myofascial Stretching: A Guide to Self-Treatment.* 2nd ed. Greenwood Village, CO: ECKO House, 2008. Print.

Another book filled with self-care techniques and lots of pictures to guide you.

books on healing

Fraser, Heather Doyle. *Daily Gratitude and Intention Journal: An Abundant Life.* Createspace, 2013. Print.

This is the journal I use to enhance my daily gratitude practice.

Emoto, Masaru. *The Hidden Messages in Water.* Hillsboro, OR: Beyond Words Pub, 2004. Print.

Fascinating pictures that clearly demonstrate how our thoughts and feelings impact the world around us.

Emoto, Masaru. *Water Crystal Healing: Music and Images to Restore Your Well-Being.* New York: Atria, 2006. Print.

> *Pictures of water crystals matched with classical music that offer a deep healing. The book comes with two CDs (note the electronic book versions do not come with the CDs).*

Levine, Peter A. *Waking the Tiger: Healing Trauma.* The Innate Capacity to Transform Overwhelming Experiences. Berkeley, CA: North Atlantic, 1997. Print.

> *An exploration of healing physical and emotional trauma using the body's innate wisdom.*

Lipton, Bruce H. *The Biology of Belief: Unleashing the Power of Consciousness,* Matter and Miracles. Santa Rosa, CA: Mountain of Love/Elite, 2005. Print.

> *Scientific work demonstrating how our thoughts and feelings impact our cells.*

Luckman, Sol. *Potentiate Your DNA: A Practical Guide to Healing & Transformation with the Regenetics Method.* Print.

> *A simple, elegant system of personal empowerment and healing using sound.*

Northrup, Christiane. *Goddesses Never Age: The Secret Prescription for Radiance, Vitality, and Well-Being.* Hay House, Inc., 2015. Print.

> *I am a big fan of all of her books; they offer tips for both men and women on embodying joy and radiance regardless of age. This latest book parallels many concepts mentioned in "*Return to Ease: Gently Reconnect with Your Body's Natural Mobility and Joy,*" including the entrapment of emotional and physical stresses in fascial restrictions.*

Oswald, Yvonne. *Every Word Has Power: Switch on Your Language and Turn on Your Life.* New York: Atria/Beyond Words Pub., 2008. Print.

> *The words you choose, both silently and vocally, can empower or dis-empower you. Change your words and you can change your life.*

Pert, Candace B. *Molecules of Emotion: Why You Feel the Way You Feel.* New York, NY: Scribner, 1997. Print.

Pioneering work on how our thoughts and emotions affect our bodies.

Smith, Douglas A. *Happiness: The Art of Living with Peace, Confidence and Joy.* Columbus, OH: White Pine Mountain, 2014. Print.

An authentic sharing of the author's path of the heart, with insights and tips to reclaiming joy in our lives.

nutritional support

Douglas Fleckman, CCN: www. douglasfleckman.com

What we ingest has the power to heal us or cause havoc within. We are biochemically unique from each other and need a personalized approach to our nutritional requirements. Working with a professional nutritionist can empower you and help your return to ease. It wasn't until I worked with Douglas that I began to thrive.

supporting products

Ordering a soft Foam Roller and a Super Pinky Ball

OPTP (Orthopedic Physical Therapy Products): www.optp.com

OPTP offers many high-quality, therapeutic tools. The self-care items used in this book are the OPTP Soft PRO-ROLLER™ the Super Pinky Ball.

Return to Ease Website: www.return2ease.com

Here you will find links to ordering the recommended products. You can also download a free MP3 file of the Body Scan Meditation set to soothing piano music.

To see clearly,

often it is necessary

to close our eyes and

engage the right brain.

— Sol Luckman

Potentiate Your DNA

I wish to personally thank the following people for their contributions to my inspiration and their assistance in creating this book:

Kevin Barnes

Matt Barnes (model)

Amelia Barnes (model)

Dave and Joan Barnes

John F. Barnes, PT

Brian Briggs, DC

Rosemary Cathcart

Michelle Clawson

Douglas Fleckman, CCN

Heather Doyle Fraser (creative development editor)

Kimberly Hill

Kim Larosa (model)

Chuck Markulis, DC

Sandee and Bill McMullen

Catherine Murray (studio shoot photographer)

Martha Somes (copy editor)

Ted Somes

Heath Sunkle (model)

Barb Swartz, Design One Graphic Design

Laura Walker

All of my beloved clients

acknowledgements

index of photographs

Cover Photo and Page 131
Title: Oregon Blue
by Catherine Murray
Location: Yachats, Oregon, USA

Page 5
Description: Denali reflection
by Greg Whiteley
Location: Alaska, USA

Page 9
Title: Serenity
by Megan Bohlander
Location: Cleveland Botanical Gardens
Cleveland, Ohio, USA

Page 13
Description: rainforest floor
by Greg Whiteley
Location: Olympic National Park
Washington, USA

Page 19
Description: bison in snow
by Greg Whiteley
Location: Yellowstone National Park, USA

Page 37
Title: Snowy Sunrise
by Roberta Kayne
Location: Bryce Canyon National Park
Utah, USA

Page 43
Description: moose in wetlands
by Greg Whiteley
Location: Kootenai National Wildlife Refuge
Idaho, USA

Page 51
Title: Sunflower and Lavender
by Roberta Kayne
Location: Valensole, Provence, France

Page 59
Description: autumn tundra
by Greg Whiteley
Location: Alaska, USA

Page 65
Title: Cliff and Sea Near Portmagee
by Roberta Kayne
Location: Portmagee, Ireland

Page 73
Description: brown bear fishing for salmon
by Greg Whiteley
Location: Alaska, USA

Page 83
Description: coral reef
by Greg Whiteley
Location: Solomon Islands, Indonesia

Page 97
Description: active volcano
by Greg Whiteley
Location: Hawaii, USA

Page 109
Description: tropical river
by Greg Whiteley
Location: Bali, Indonesia

Page 123
Description: bugling elk
by Greg Whiteley
Location: Jasper, BC, Canada

Pages 15, 21, 39, 75 and 125
Title: Sunrise in the White Mountains
by Roberta Kayne
Location: New Hampshire, USA

Photographers:

Megan Bohlander
www.bohlanderphotography.com

Roberta Kayne
www.KaynePhotography.com

Catherine Murray
www.photokitchen.net

Greg Whiteley
www.spiritinthelight.com